T0198892

The Pearl of Life:

A MAN'S JOURNEY

By Eric D. Maze

To order additional copies of this book, contact:
Xlibris
844-714-8691
www.Xlibris.com
Orders@Xlibris.com

ISBN: Softcover   978-1-4134-6569-3

Print information available on the last page

Rev. date: 07/05/2022

My name is Eric D. Maze and I am an aspiring poet that works for the State of New Jersey taking care of blind, deaf, and mute mentally disable individuals. I have decided to write this poetry book to tell my story. The book is separated into different sections according to different aspects of my life. We all go through changes and life changes. In this book I have written different poems that represented a time period in my life that have altered my life forever.

Growing up I have always written poetry as a way of expressing how I felt inside. I was always too shy to tell others how I felt. Well these poems are very personal; but then again every poem is personal. A good poem is always personal and comes from the heart. There are so many critics out there that criticize how poems are written and what style they are written in. Whatever happened to writing poetry from our hearts? The classic versions of rhyming with the beat of our hearts. I don't claim to be a great poet; I just want to be heard.

The main reason I wrote this poetry book is to give to all of my friends a remembrance of me when I am no longer on this earth. If poetry readers are a lot like me, then you wouldn't really care who wrote it, you would just like to read it because it is poetry. That is the true love of the poetry word.

The book is a little piece of me that I want to give to the world. It is for my friends, family, and whoever wishes to read it. We all go through life changes and remember what happened at the time, but do we ever have something to remind us of that time period? Most likely the answer is no. Well in this book you do. Even though it is my life, I am sure we can all transfer what happened to me to what has happened to you.

I had fun writing this book, and fun remembering all that life has given to me in my life. I hope that you will enjoy the poems because they are for your pleasure. Growing up I have always been told the main reason why people don't like poetry is simply because they don't understand them. Well that is why I made this book the way it is. It explains each poem and the time period in my life at the time. So many people are turned off from poetry because they don't understand them. Hopefully you will come to appreciate poems more from this book because poetry is a beautiful language on its own that makes the world around us look a whole lot better.

A poetry world is a world of wonder and mystique. It celebrates life to its fullest capacity. I hope you enjoy this poetry book and enjoy my poetry world. Thank you for choosing to enter what is going to be a journey. A journey into life and life changes, a journey that will take you into a world of wonder and magic. Again, thank you for stepping into my poetry world . . . ENJOY . . .

LIFE CHANGES AND REBIRTH OF A

NEW PERSON

(Sometimes the results are better than the journey)

HEAVEN'S STREAM

AS THE STREAM FLOWS INTO THE EVERGREEN,

AN ECLIPSING MOON SHINNING ITS BEAM,
DEVOURS ITSELF INTO MY TEARY EYES,
MEMORIES CLUTTER MY MIND AS I SWEEP MY TEARS
DRY,
TIME, AS I KNOW IT, DIMINISHES INTO THE NIGHT.

A MIRAGE OF SYMBOLS DASH BEFORE ME,
AS I MUST DEFER TO MY MIND WITHOUT DEGREE.
LET THE TEARS COME WHEN I HAVE NO WHERE ELSE
TO FALL.
FOR IT IS THE SPIRIT WITHIN THAT KEEPS US ALIVE
AND TALL.
THE RIVER HOLDS MY SOUL IN A CRYSTALLIZE BALL
OF LIGHT.

IN THE PALM OF MY HAND I HOLD THE POWER,
THE POWER WITHIN THE SOUL THAT KEEPS THE
TOWER.
THE TOWER WITHIN MY HEART SHIELDS ITS LONELY
MASK,
AS THE MASK CRUMBLES INTO THE DARK DUST AT
LAST.
AND SO, THE *NEW WORLD* SHALL BEGIN IN MY HEART
AND THE UNICORN IS IN FLIGHT . . .

LET THE DREAMS BEGIN ANEW,
A FACE OF LIFE IN THE SHADOWS OF THE DEW.
WITH EVERY OUNCE OF MY SOUL AND LIFE,
SHALL THE *NEW WORLD* BEGIN ITS FLIGHT?

"Heaven's Stream" was a poem I wrote free hand at a time in my life when a lot of changes were going on. I had to make a lot of hard decisions that would effect the rest of my life. The decisions were leaving my job and leaving my family to move in my own house.

Time went on and I decided to move out of the house that I lived with my parents, but was still having a hard time leaving my job. I guess the reason why I was and still having a hard time leaving my job is because of all the friends I have met in the years I have been there and the fact that I still care for the Individuals as if they were my own children. The most precious part of my life is my friends. Especially, after suffering the lost of most of my friends in my early years.

Over time it has seemed that my co—workers—friends have gotten pretty close to me. I dare say that they even may know me better than I understand myself at times. I can't possibly see leaving these loyal friends. One thing that I have learned is that no matter what will happen these loyal friends will be with me for the rest of my life. As time changes, so do we; but we still have a tendency to be with each other no matter what. There is no amount of money in the world that can tear me away from my friends. Friendship is the most important thing in my life. Money is not everything. Being happy at what you do, and having friends that you can count on means everything.

I have felt so much pain in my life to want to go back to the past. Having two friends, and having both of my Grandparents die made it a very hard time for me to get close to people. Over the years I have learned to get close, but I have learned that it takes time for me to do so.

I have learned a lot throughout the years while maintaining a steady job. Lessons that I will cherish for the rest of my life. For this I typed the poem "Heaven's Stream" for moving on in my life and allowing me to become the best person I could ever be in life. This poem shows me moving on in my life while conquering struggles that came about at the time and allowing them to finally be an appearance of Heaven flowing through "Heaven's Stream".

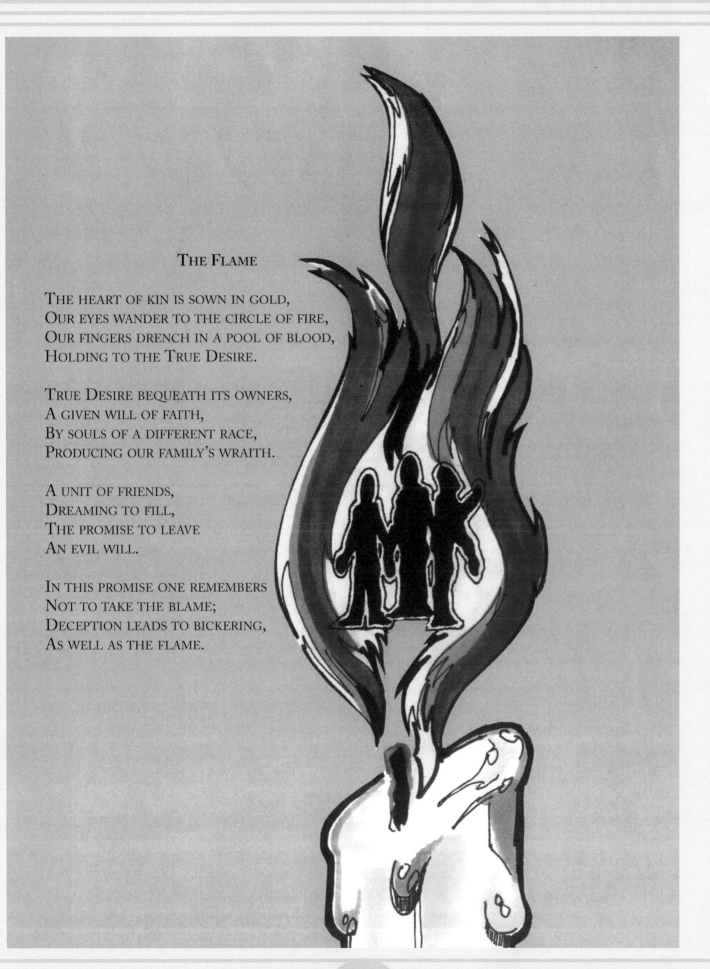

The Flame

The heart of kin is sown in gold,
Our eyes wander to the circle of fire,
Our fingers drench in a pool of blood,
Holding to the True Desire.

True Desire bequeath its owners,
A given will of faith,
By souls of a different race,
Producing our family's wraith.

A unit of friends,
Dreaming to fill,
The promise to leave
An evil will.

In this promise one remembers
Not to take the blame;
Deception leads to bickering,
As well as the flame.

The poem "The Flame" was a poem I had written for the suspense story I had written back in the summer of 1992. The story was entitled "The Gray Flame". Now that I look at the poem I've come to realize that it can be taken in different meanings when read. What the poem really was saying, or meant to say is no matter what hard times shall fall upon us we should always be able to count on our friends at all times. In a sense that is what "The Gray Flame" really represented.

"The Flame" actually was going to be thrown away by me, but something inside of me told me not to. I kept it for the future. In a way this poem was the inspiration that kept me writing the other poems over the years. I know there are not a lot of them, but they all have a significant meaning to me, and I would like to share them with you. Writing poetry was just a hobby for me and still is. I really don't have the desire to be famous or want a lot of money; I just want my word to be heard. That is why this poetry book is mainly for my friends and anybody who wishes to read my poems or words.

Life is the most precious thing we have and when we have a tendency to feel bad we, as a whole, tend to forget the most important things in life. Even the worst of things can be the best of things. To make a mistake is human; to learn from that mistake is wise. We wouldn't be human if we didn't make mistakes. It is our reactions and emotions that distinguish us as Individuals. To error is to learn, and to learn is to be born. So, please don't apologize for a mistake, just learn from that mistake so that it never happens again.

Let your knowledge be your guide to teaching the children by setting an example, a positive action that they can understand. If they realize that an adult can make a mistake, then they will never feel bad about themselves and will want to succeed in what ever they may want to do without the pressure of failure mounting on their backs. Too much anger at themselves for not succeeding will only allow them to grow up with low self esteem, which will come back to haunt them later in life. Everybody must realize that it is not whether you win or lose the game; it is how you play the game. Know it, live it, and do it. The word is mightier than the sword. Sometimes, The word can be the most hurtful to a person.

The Ghostly Rose

A dark sky pierces through the eclipse,
As shadow people escapes through the air in sequence.
My mind whispers out tears of faces,
One by one they lapse in and out of places.

Thundering rain echoing to the ground,
Crashing like lightening while tracing my face abound.
My face trenched in an overflow river,
Sweep against the tide of my face as a drifter.

Tears rolling as memories dance,
Of a family fades in a trance.
A Ghostly Rose falls from my windowsill,
As a mirage of a Mother's face appears in ill.

The Ghostly Rose glides it's way to the ground,
As my years with my mother are soon to be found.
Trembling to the ground the Ghostly Rose appears,
As so my heart had fallen in a river of tears.

So long my mother for I have no fear,
Some day I will be near.
The Ghostly Rose will soon reappear,
In the garden of love in full sincere.

"The Ghostly Rose" was a poem I wrote in remembrance of my grandmother when she was alive. My grandmother and I were very close. She died from a massive heart attack. It was the first and the last one that she had. It was the first time I had experienced death, and it was the hardest one I have ever dealt with. When a person at such a young age has to deal with the lost of not one, but both of your grandparents it makes you grow up even faster than you should have.

My grandmother taught me a lot about my family history, and about how to use your creativity to make something out of nothing at all. I remember one time when my brothers and I made a grill outside out of cylinder blocks and wood. Believe or not, we were able to do it. It was great!

In the poem "The Ghostly Rose" I am remembering my grandmother and think about how the feeling of my own mother felt when my grandmother died. The hardest thing in the world is when you have to bury a parent that you love so dearly. Although, I do not fully understand how it feels, I can allow my own feelings for my grandmother transcend into how my mother's feelings were at that time. It may not be the same, but it is close enough. Everybody goes through a death in their family that hits them the hardest and changes them for the rest of their lives. My grandmother's death was mine. It was a time when I knelt down by her casket and vowed to honor her forever and to always remember the lessons that she taught me. Till this day, I hold that promise. I will always strive to be the best I could be.

Later in years, I learned that this promise was a promise that kept me still holding onto my grandmother and not letting her go to heaven. In the year 2001 I let her go. I finally learned something that I would tell others, but was not following myself. The lesson was everybody is allowed to fail, including me. I had always kept that promise as a way of never failing. I didn't allow myself to fail. When I did fail I would put myself into a depression because I broke my promise to my grandmother. Today, I've come to realize that my grandmother just wanted me to TRY TO DO MY BEST, NOT BE THE BEST. The promise ended and I was finally a complete person on the inside. Another lesson that I learned from this was we all must learn to let go the ones we love. It is selfish of us to hold onto them and not let them be free. We should never forget them in our hearts, but we must let go and continue to live our lives the way they wanted us to. It is always hard to let go of someone you love. In this poem my remembrance of my grandmother is set free for you to read. God Bless you Grandma, I love you and will always miss you.

FATHER

FATHER I MUST CONFESS,
ALL THE LOVE YOU HAVE SHOWN I MUST DISTRESS.
LIFE HAS DEALT ME THE HAND TO LEAVE THE NEST.
BUT, I CAN'T WITHOUT BRINGING OUT SOMETHING TO REST.

GROWING UP I DID NOT KNOW THE TRUE WEALTH WITHIN YOUR HEART,
YEARS AND DAYS ARE GONE NOW KNOWING THAT YOU WERE THERE FROM THE START.
HOW I LONG TO BRING YESTERDAY BACK,
BUT, I KNOW YOU CAN NOT RETRACT.

SILENT TEARS ARE SWEPT AWAY,
FOR A MAN IS HERE TO STAY.
PAST IS GONE, TOMORROW IS HERE.
HAPPINESS FILLS MY HEART WITH KNOWLEDGE THAT YOU CARE.

YOU ARE IN MY TENDER HEART, RIGHT WHERE YOU BELONG,
TOGETHER WE WILL BE STRONG.
REMEMBER MY WORDS WHEN WE CAN NOT BE,
I LOVE YOU TO THE END OF ETERNITY.

The poem "Father" was a poem I had written when I was moving out of the house that I lived in with my parents. It was a poem I dedicated to my father who has always been there for me. Growing up he worked two jobs and was in the military. I never saw him when I was growing up. The time that I saw him was on the weekends when he came home to sleep. As I became a teenager, I became his best friend. I grew into a young man and slowly got closer to my father. I finally knew who he was.

I've come to realize that in this world every parent makes a sacrifice that has a consequence on his or her family. It takes time to replenish that sacrifice as the years pass by. Boys are told to never show emotion, but as men we finally learn that showing emotion only makes us human. My father never really had a chance to have a family. His family was my mother's family. He has very unusual behaviors, but as I watch him and realize it is his past that has taught him to behave in these strange manners. You can not blame a person for their faults of which they have learned from a family that wasn't present. Over the years he has learned to love his family, friends, and people that he meets. It is because of my mother that he has learned to become a better person.

I have learned what true love is through watching my parents. When the worst of times come, it is your mate that is there to care and comfort you through it all. Your mate is the one that takes the blame and accepts all of your faults and still loves you no matter what. My parents are very much in love with each other now as much as they were since the first day they met. Its not what is on the outside of a person, but on the inside of a person that makes the relationship last forever.

When I made the poem "Father" I was thinking of my father and how I have just started to know who he really was. It was a time I was moving out of my parents' house into my new house on my own. I didn't want to forget my dad. I wanted to still maintain the love and friendship that I developed once I became an Adult. I had lost too many years with my father when I was growing up, so I didn't want to go back to that situation again just because I was moving out on my own. I love my father and will always be there for him. I hope when people read this poem they realize just because you're a man doesn't mean that you can't still admit that you love your father. I hope that some day people will realize how precious their fathers really are, and learn to cherish them because not everybody in this world has one. Special men are a rarity, unfortunately. We should honor them, not neglect them.

Mom

My wings are flapping in the wind,
Don't cry Mom for I will not sin.
When I was a child you taught me right from wrong.
Now it is time for me to write a new song.

I remember when you held me when I cried,
You stayed up and watch me lie.
You made me strong and ready for the fight,
But, what you didn't know was all right.

Don't cry for all is right,
I'll remember you tonight.
When the wind blows and echoes your name,
I'll be there calling just the same.

Lonely as I am in this big world,
I'll remember you as a shinning pearl.
You glitter with gold in your eyes,
Your dazzling smile sweeps through the sky.

Many miles away,
And still I can not say,
The words I said as a child I once knew,
The words: I love you.

The poem "Mom" was a poem that I made for my mother. It was a poem that I dedicated to my mother after all of the great things that she had done for me in my life. There is nothing I could ever do to mount up to the kind of love and dedication that she gave me when I was growing up.

I was born with a very rare condition that was only treated in the early 70's. I have what is known as phenylketonuria (PKU). It is known as a disease of metabolism because the children with the disease can't use a common protein food product called phenylanine. The abnormal metabolism that is the cause of this disease if untreated will lead to mental retardation. It begins at the age of birth and if not treated by the time the child is one year old it will lead to mental retardation.

With the help of a team of doctors and my mother I was treated in time to save me from any severe disabilities. Often these children are withdrawn and very difficult to handle because of behavior problems; of which I thank God didn't have. The one thing I did find myself being withdrawn to myself and sometimes depressed. Over the years I have learned to fight these things off when they do sneak up on me. There was a pink formula that I was made to drink as a supplement for the lack of protein in my life. If I didn't have any protein I would not have been able to grow. There is only a certain amount of protein I can intake on a daily basis. Despite my constant refusal to drink the formula, my mother would not give up on me. My father would try to sneak cookies and ice cream cake to eat, but my mother would catch him and take it away from me. It is because of this persistence by her that I was able to live a normal life without any severe mental disabilities. My mother saved my life.

Every year I spent taking psychological tests from team of doctors and weekly blood tests from my infant stage to the age of twelve. I never had a birthday cake until I was five years old when my mother brought one in to celebrate with my classmates. It wasn't ice cream, but it was the greatest Mickey Mouse cake a little kid could ever have. Till this day, I still remember that cake.

At the age of twelve, I told my doctors and my mother that I wanted off of the diet. My doctors and mother warned me of the consequences of such action, but my mother trusted me and believed in me. I was able to go off of the diet, but with the doctors promise that I would watch everything I ate during the daytime and nighttime, so I wouldn't have an episode of twitches, or sickness. With the love of my mother, I was able to be free to a somewhat normal life.

I love my mother; not in ways a normal boy loves his mother; but in ways of a boy loves life. I would not be alive today if it weren't for my mother; SHE SAVED MY LIFE. I would do anything for my mother, for she is my soul, my life, and my love. And I do mean it literally.

This poem was dedicated to you mom: I LOVE YOU MOM. AND I WILL ALWAYS LOVE YOU FOREVER.

THE RIVER MAN

TRAVELING DOWN A RIVER WATCHING THE WAVES,
A MAN STANDS BEFORE THE ETERNAL CAVES.
FACES THAT HAUNT HIM ARE THE FACES THAT HE FEEDS,
ONE BY ONE ARE THE MOUTHS HE SEEDS.

SITTING BY THE TREE, I CRY AT THE KNOWLEDGE OF THIS MAN,
BECAUSE I KNOW EVERYTHING HE CATCHES IS ONLY IN A CAN.
AS THE MAN WALKS BESIDE ME, I OFFER HIM A HAND,
BUT HE TURNS TO ME AND SAYS I CAN NOT ACCEPT, FOR I AM HEADING TO MY LAND.

AS I TURNED AND WATCHED, THE MAN IN THE RIVER'S EYES,
LIKE DIAMONDS AND PEARLS, DISSOLVED INTO THE WATER'S TIDES.
IN A SECOND OF WONDER,
THE MAN IN THE RIVER BECAME ONE WITH THE WATER.

SITTING BY THE TREE,
I STARED AT THE SEA,
ONLY TO DISCOVER AN ANGEL FLYING TO THE SKY,
ESCAPING FROM THE WATER'S CRASHING TIDE.

THAT NIGHT I SAT BY THE TREE, AND LOOKED OUT TO THE SEA,
ONLY TO DISCOVER THE MAN IN THE RIVER'S CHILDREN OF THREE.
ONE BY ONE THEY FELL INTO THE RIVER,
NEVER TO RESURFACE FROM THE HOUR.

I WATCHED AND DISCOVERED,
THREE ANGELS HAD FINALLY BEEN RECOVERED.
TOGETHER THEY FOLLOW TO BE WITH THEIR FATHER.
THIS TREE OF DEATH NEAR THIS WATER,
BEGONE WITH THE ANGELS AND THEIR FATHER.

SITTING BY THE TREE, I CRY.
THE MAN IN THE RIVER I CAN SEE IN THE SKY.
WHAT BEAUTIFUL FACES HAUNT ME IN THIS SEA?
AS I SIT BY THE TREE.

The poem "The River Man" is a very special poem for me. I chant this poem by the lake that I grew up next to. It helps me remember what is important in life, and it helps me stay grounded and aware of my surroundings. It shows me that you can't give people the easy way out of life, you have to allow them to grow in their life. You have to let them make their own mistakes and to allow them to become their true selves. Even though I can see some friends heading in the wrong direction, I know that by experience in my own life that you must let them find the answers to their own problems. I can't tell them where to go, but I can help them along the way to the right direction in their lives. I don't know everything, and it would be a crime to think that I did. I am still learning in my life. I will probably be learning new things for the rest of my life. The day I stop learning will be the day I die. One who lives, but doesn't learn is a fool to life: a wasted life. The only reason why I think I might be able to help is simply because of the problems I have endured in my life. I can; however, pass along what I learned from my mistakes to another so that person doesn't make the same mistake.

Because we are humans, we are prone to make mistakes. The problem is did you learn from your mistake, or are you doomed to keep repeating the same mistake? That is the question one must ask in their lives. I don't have all the answers, and please don't look to me for them. The answers, I have learned, are within each one of us. We are the masters of our own destiny. It is you who make the decisions and it is you that receive the consequences of each action that you take. Just make sure that you analyze each action before you take it, so that you don't feel tied down to a consequence that you don't want.

This poem is special to me, because of what it represents to me. One of the things we should always remember is that no matter what kind of problems we have in our lives there is always somebody else in this world that has it worse than you. Don't ever take your life for granted because it is the most precious thing in this world. Every one of us is special on the inside. This poem to me reminds me of just that idea and belief. In my eyes everybody is special, even the ones we hate.

<u>ROMANTIC LESSONS</u>
<u>OF THE</u>

<u>HEART</u>

(You always learn from the ones you love)

FRIENDSHIP

A HORSE IN THE FIELD STANDING BY THE WATER FILLED WITH MAGICAL DUST,
ITS EMERALD EYES GLARE AT THE SKY ABOVE THE WANDERLUST.
DANCING ANGELS FALL FROM THE SKY,
WHAT A DELIGHTFUL SIGHT TO MY EYE.

THE HORSE GALLOPS INTO THE WATER TO BE FREE,
AS CRYSTAL DROPS SEEM TO FALL INTO THE BREEZE.
STARS ABOVE AND BEYOND RECITE YOUR TORRENTIAL CALM,
LET THE ANGELS COME FROM HEAVEN'S PALM.

EMERALD EYES WITHIN THE SKY OF THE NIGHT,
RELEASE THE ANGELS' POWER OF MIGHT.
IN THE WHISPER OF THE WIND,
COMES A STRANGER FROM WITHIN.

STARS ABOVE THE NIGHT,
ALLOW ME TO COME TONIGHT.
THIS STRANGER WITHIN MY SIGHT,
HAS BECOME A FRIEND FOR LIFE.

The poem "Friendship" is a poem I wrote about a friend that came into my life almost out of thin air. She is a very special friend that means a lot to me. When we first met it was in a time of sorrow for her. A comforting smile and a reassuring word of praise warmed her heart. Her lost was replaced by my friendship by accident. We talked and talked, realizing that there was a lot in common between the two of us.

This poem represents the emergence of our friendship at a time she had lost somebody very close to her heart. Every time I look into her eyes I see the beauty within her, even though I know her lack of self—esteem prevents her from thinking that. The poem "Friendship" was the first time in my life I came to an understanding that friendship was the most potent force on earth. It was also the first time I realized that in order to love a person you must be their friend first.

Friendship is the doorway to many avenues in my life, especially romance. I have come to realize that the one characteristic I'm looking for in a woman is simply a friend I can laugh with, cry with, and have conversations with. The poem was a time period in my life when I realized what I was looking for in a woman: a woman that I would like to marry.

In all of the years before, I have never thought of what kind of woman I was looking for. The poem "Friendship" has special meaning to me, because it represented a special friend that showed me what I was looking for in a woman. A friendship that developed over the years that I hold very close to my heart.

THE PURPLE ROSE

A SOFT PETAL TWINKLES IN THE WIND,
AS THE TENDER CHEEK TOUCHES MY SKIN IN SIN.
SWEET AROMA LIGHTS UP MY LIFE,
AS HER MAGICAL TOUCH AROUSES MY SOUL LIKE A KNIFE.

THE STEM OF HER BODY CARESSES MINE,
UP AND DOWN AND ALL AROUND LIKE THE KISS OF FINE WINE.
SILKY MOISTURE GLISTENS ON THE BREASTS OF A WOMAN IN LOVE,
THE APPEARANCE OF VELVET ROSE LYING ON TOP OF HER LIKE A GLOVE.

WILD FIRE EYES STARRING INTO MINE WHILE THE TEMPERATURE FLARES,
EXPLORING HANDS FALL INTO PLACES WHERE THE UNKNOWN DARES.
A MAGICAL ENTRANCE IS PIERCED BY THE GOLDEN KNIFE,
IN AND OUT WITH A SURE PROTECTION OF NO LIFE.

THE MOONLIGHT SOFTENS THE LIGHT ON A WOMAN IN REST,
A ROSE ON TOP REFLECTS NOTHING BUT THE BEST.
A PURPLE ROSE STAYS ON TOP FOR THE WORLD TO SEE,
ON THE INSIDE OF A WOMAN IS THE HEART OF GOLD FLOATING IN THE HIDDEN SEA.

The poem "The Purple Rose" was a poem that will always stay in my head forever. I wrote this poem when I first started dating a woman that I grew very fond of. In its essence were my true feelings at the time whenever I was near her. She brought new feelings into my life that will always stay with me. At the time, I was having feelings that I had never had my entire life.

The one true thing I learned through this was love could bring the best out of people. Whenever I was with her, or near her, I always was and still am at my best. It was the first time I felt the true mighty power of LOVE. The relationship started out rather slowly, as friends. The friendship grew into love, and became the greatest love I had ever known. It is true in that old saying of "patience is a virtual". This relationship showed me this.

This was a time in my life when everything was really great. Many lessons have been learned from this relationship and still to this day. She filled my heart and my life with the utmost love that I have a hard time describing. I know as the future continues that I will keep on learning from her. It is because of her that I have grown into the man that I am today.

"The Purple Rose" stays with me as I remember the days we were together. Everybody in this world has a soul mate. I truly believe this. I didn't quite believe it when I was a teenager. I had always thought that there was nobody for me. I never thought that anybody would be able to understand me or let a lone able to match me. Do I believe in soul mates? Yes, I do. I think that I just found mine. Thank you God for blessing me with mine. Soul mates last a lifetime; they don't walk away when you need them. They go through the trials and tribulations that you go through in your life. They are always there for you.

As I have grown I have learned that love transcends through all hate and bitterness. You must respect each other and love each other, even your enemies. It is a fool that can not respect others. Fools are the ones that are always hurting themselves. When you are at peace with yourself others know it. Many of my enemies or adversaries have tried there hardest to put me down and do some nasty things to me, but I have learned to turn the other cheek. I can not and will not allow them to tarnish my spirit. I will love and not hate them. This in turn will only frustrate them and stop them from attacking me. I have learned this over the years. Surprisingly, this has always worked.

Love, as in the bible, shows us that it is the most powerful feeling in the world. Through experiences in my life and through my relationships I have learned that it truly is. The poem "The Purple Rose" has a very significant meaning to me. It reminded me that LOVE is truly the most powerful weapon in the world. Those who hate and are bitter lose the ability to think clearly. A loving heart goes on forever and ever . . . Truly the most powerful weapon in the world!

LADY MYSTIQUE

Red velvet eyes lurk through the Smokey air,
Rising above the murky clouds appears the tender mare.
Gallant streams of gold flicker in hope,
As criss cross rays devour and elope.

The mind of madness separates into a mindless mishap,
Calmness invades the serenity of being entrapped.
Streaks of hope fall into a pot of gold,
Allowing only the spirit that has become bold.

The mare allows itself to take that first step,
A step of independence, a step that is left unkempt.
Future plans and future dreams,
Is all of that what is left to be filled in the gold of streams?

Fly my angel and don't let go.
A mare soon to be an angel in the golden flow.
What appears to my eyes but a tender woman's face?
A woman's face filled with a soft, tender body of lace.

The poem "Lady Mystique" is a poem that is about a mysterious lady that came into my life. This mysterious lady became a best friend and lover. The reason why this poem has special meaning is because this mysterious lady went through a life change while I knew her. In front of my own eyes she grew up to become a full bloom woman that her parents would be very proud of.

This poem reminds me of the many changes that we go through in our lives. There are many changes that we must go through to become the person that we were meant to become. Many people ask me these simple questions, "Why? Haven't I gone through enough changes in my life? Why does everything happen to me?"

I can't say that I have all the answers to these questions, but I can tell what I have learned through careful study of people's lives throughout my years. I've always had a curious mind when it comes to the way people handle the many difficulties in life. Even when I was a child many people came to me for answers to their problems. For example, I once had a friend whose sister was raped by their father, and didn't know what to do or how to handle it. Also, I had a friend who was the most popular person in school and kept asking for my advice on how to handle his girlfriend when they were breaking up. The advice I gave him worked and helped them get back together as a couple. I guess in a way you could say that I have been helping people my whole life. So, when people ask me these questions, I take them very seriously and try to come up with an answer for them to the best of my ability.

Through the years I have learned that we all go through trials and tribulations to test us and to make us into better people. Sometimes the reason why these tragedies happen is because somewhere down the road we were all at one point in time heading down the wrong road and we were too blind to see the truth. It is these tragedies that wakes us up to what we are doing wrong in our lives and God gives us another chance to correct the things that we got wrong and change our direction to bigger and better things in our lives. Yes, there are many things that happen that make us feel that we are cursed to bad luck, but the reality of it all is quite simple. There are always different paths in our lives we choose to take; the question is which one should we take? Too many times we allow our negatively take control of our lives and make us feel that there is only one path to take, when the truth is that there are many paths to take you just have to open your eyes to all of them and decide.

The poem "Lady Mystique" is very important to me because of what it symbolizes to this mysterious woman and the symbolism it represents in life as well. You should always remember to look at all of the paths and decide. You should not think that there is only one path for you to take in life, or you will end up taking the wrong path in life. God gives man the freedom of free will: we should all use it wisely; not use it disparagingly like a lot of us have done in the past.

<u>NATURE</u>

(In order to be a complete person one must learn from Mother Nature.)

SHE HAS ALL OF THE ANWSERS TO LIFE, JUST LISTEN TO HER.

THE MOON IN THE SEA

THE DARK MOON REACHES THE SEA,
MY SHADOW REACHES OUT FOR ME.
TIME IS OF ESSENCE TO THE SOUL,
WHY THEN MUST THESE TESTS TAKE THEIR TOLL?

CARESSING WAVES SPLATTER AMONG THE LAIR,
ECHOES OF SEA GULLS WHISPER IN MY EAR WITHIN ME I MUST BARE.
A DARK CRESCENT MOON BECKONS TO ME IN THE FLOWING WAVES,
HOWLING OUT THE SEA'S STORIES I REMEMBER SO CLEARLY IN NAME.

ONE BY ONE THE VISIONS REAPPEAR IN QUESTION,
FOR IT IS THE SEA IN THE MOON CRASHING INTO THE BEACH IN AGGRESSION.
WHAT AILS THE BROKEN HEART ON THIS STRICKEN NIGHT?
MEMORIES OF STORIES THAT ARE TOLD IN THE LIGHT ARE BROUGHT TONIGHT.

THE CRESCENT MOON STARES BACK WITHOUT QUESTION FROM THE SEA.
A WANDERING MIND CAN EASE OF STORIES OF THREE.
COLD AND MILKY SAND TOUCHES MY TOES AS THE WAVES CRASH BEFORE ME.
A FALLEN MOON SWEEPS ITS PRESENCE AND DRIFTS INTO SEA.

HANDS OF PASSION AND HANDS OF LIFE PRESSES,
THROUGH THE WHITE, BUBBLY FOAM OF THE WATER'S CARESSES.
VISIONS OF LOVE, AND PASSION FILL MY HEART,
MAINTAINING A PROMISE THAT I WILL NOT FALL APART.

THIS STONE WITHIN MY PALM, WITHIN MY HEART,
SHALL CRUMBLE TO THE SEA AND RENEW MY LIFE FROM THE START.
TRANSGRESSION BLAZES THROUGH THE OPEN SEA WITH AGGRESSION,
ONLY TO BE REGRESSING IN MY HEART WITH LOVE AND AFFECTION.

THE MOON IN THE SEA IS WITHIN MY SOUL,
LET THE MEMORIES PAST BEFORE ME WITHOUT ITS TOLL.
ALLOW THE DOVES TO FLY THROUGH THE WAVES,
AND ALLOW THE DOVES TO SHOW ME THE WAY.

HOWLING TO THE MOON

Nature in the eyes of its onlooker has the power to heal. The poem "The Moon in the Sea" was a poem that I wrote when I was in High School. I remember those days like it was yesterday. I would spend the nights by myself looking out to the sea skipping rocks onto the water's currents remembering my past as the years had gone by. I would spend hours sitting on the rocks starring up into the sky and wishing upon the stars for a true love and asking questions about the universe.

There is nothing better than sitting by the rocks on a cold brisk night starring into a starry night and pondering about the world's problems and why life exists. The beauty of the stars shinning upon the dark water looked like a magical waterfall scattering among the silky sand. I remember when it was dusk I would watch as the golden glimmer of the sun devoured itself into the water below. It looked like golden stars transcending into a path of gold heading to the silky sand of heaven. It was truly a place of tranquility. Many of days and nights were spent here pondering about life and experiences that I had to handle in my life.

The poem "The Moon in the Sea" was a poem that I wrote describing what I saw and how I interpreted it. The sheer beauty of the ocean allowed my soul to heal from the heartbreak of failing in life. Many times I have tried to advance myself in my life and failed. I have learned over the years that failure can change to victory. I had to learn to pick myself up and heal myself. I learned to take care of myself and listen to mother nature. If you stop and listen for a second you can hear that voice inside of you. This voice inside of you is called your conscience. Over the years I've learned if you listen to it, your life will be in good standing. That voice is your voice talking to yourself. Please, pay attention to that voice. It may not always be right, but it will help you in your time of need. If you can free your mind, you can free your soul.

Sometimes, we as humans must take the time in our lives to clear our minds and appreciate our surroundings no matter what that may be. The simplest little thing has a beauty to it we just need to take the time to see it. When everything is said and done, what in your life can you really appreciate the most? If you didn't have anything that was materialistic would life exist? Too many times we take for granted the most precious things in our lives. Would you love yourself if you didn't have these things in your life? Would you still have the same beliefs that you do now?

Nature can teach you a lot of things if you take the time to listen. For example, a simple flow of water through two rocks creates a waterway for plants and wild flowers that harness the life of insects that are eaten by birds. In this circle of life that happens everyday before your very eyes show the effect of one person has on other people. What may seem so insufficient to you may mean more to another person. If you can start the ball rolling in your life, then other events that have more of an effect in your life will result. It is the small things in life that mean the most in life. Everybody feels that they don't make a difference in this world, well this example of nature shows otherwise. We all make a difference; don't ever give up. It is when you give up that the chain of life stops. DON'T EVER GIVE UP. Love your life and its surroundings and life will love you back.

THE PASSING OF THE LEAF

Streaks of light fall within the mirror of symmetry,
Fly a rainbow of golden stars into the water,
Allow the fear that I hold inside this hollow tree,
Disperse into feelings of a mind destine to become broader.

This hollow tree grows into an evergreen,
An evergreen filled with stars of the rainbow.
The ocean around this tree holds the fears that are forever seen.
One by one these leaves of life fall into a water bowl.

Gliding off to a new life in a steam of gold,
These leaves are temples of my soul.
Take these leaves and learn to be bold,
Become the one to take control.

Swaying in and out in the stream,
Like a magical swan waiting to deliver a message.
A message of wonder in the essence of my dream.
The leaf comes to a stop from its passage.

This leaf of magic is for your pleasure,
Enjoy with delight of my knowledge that is awakening.
Allow the opening of your treasure,
Release my spirit within which is left for your taking.

The poem "The Passing of the Leaf" was written as a symbolic passage of my life entering into a new life cycle. Everybody's life changes like the new fallen seasons that occur every year. These life cycles are natural events that change our lives forever. Like butterflies in the early spring changing once the weather gets warm, my life changed as I got older. This poem was written to show the changing of life into a New World as an adult. Many things change once you get older, what you thought was right was really wrong when you got older. Mistakes made an impression on my mind that altered the way I thought. Now instead of doing an action without thinking, I think before I act. I've learned that better consequences occur when I take the time to plan and analyze the situation before I make a decision.

"The Passing of the Leaf" was a poem that showed the metamorphous that occurs in each and one of us as we get older. We must accept certain things and go on with our lives. We all must learn to leave the past behind and continue on with our lives. We must accept our past and learn from it so that we don't make the same mistake again in the future.

When I got older I realized that changes were occurring within me as well. My theories, ideas, and knowledge improved as I grew up to be an Adult. Like the changing of the leaf, my life altered me into a better person. I truly believe that as we all get older we change into the person that we were meant to become in the eyes of God. In this poem I use the symbol of a leaf falling to the ground as a metaphor for me changing into a man. The many changes and different beliefs that followed were not something I was prepared for in my life. This poem helped me understand that some changes can make you into a better person.

The Flight of the Red Tail Hawk

Angels flock to the sky,
Howling wind echoes out the name I long to hear.
A crumbling tower of fear awakens in my eye,
As tremors of laughter echoes in my ear.

As the hawk comes near,
A darken sky follows the light.
In one long swoop the flash of remembrance comes in tears.
Gallant streams of shadows fall within the night.

How I hunger to hold and caress the wildness within,
Only to behold the ghost of my soul.
Scented aroma ripples through my nose and tickles like a petal's rim.
A long caressing touch of your skin allowing my body to fall.

Dodging through trees, enjoying the breeze.
Love so tender that it awakens the darken night.
You were always full of fun and a delightful tease.
How I long for your beautiful sight.

In one flicker of the moon,
I knew the darkness of the night comes to light.
The reality of awakening shall return soon.
Remembrance will now pass through the flight.

All the dreams that pass before me are all past.
Now I have grown in the dark wilderness.
I have finally found peace at last.
Thanks to my friends' helpful willingness.

The poem "The Flight of Red Tail Hawk" was a poem that I wrote when I was sitting by a lake that I grew up by. In the sky I would watch how the birds flew in a V—shape form. I could always tell who the leader of the group of birds was. On those nights that I watched the sunset and watched as the birds flew off into the sunset I would remember all of the past friends that have come and gone in my life. The leader of the birds always directed the pact into the sunset, while other leaders stayed on the ground relaxing in the water.

I always thought of the birds as a group of friends that would always stick together. They seemed to never depart from each other. A part of me always envied that about them. It was at a time in my life when I was graduating High School and all of my friends had left me. The majority of them went to College, or moved out of state. So I spent a lot of time by the water and watch the birds set off into the sunset.

This poem meant a lot to me because it allowed me to disappear into my own world as one of those birds. How I had longed to fly through the sky without anything holding me back; a reality that set me free in a world that seemed so harsh. Everybody has a secret place where they go to let their mind free from all the worries of the world. This lake was my freedom. An Escape into a magical world as I felt the breeze hit my face and the sand creep into my toes as I sat by the lake watching the sunset. The beautiful colors lit up the sky like a movie playing every night with the birds being the main attraction.

FUN POEMS

(ALL WORK AND NO PLAY MAKES FOR A DULL PERSON)

YOU ONLY LIVE ONCE, SO WHY NOT ENJOY IT?

Terror of the Night

Ghastly ghouls spread the news,
A pricey head for all the clues.
One finger, two ears, and one eye in the sky,
Fall from my mouth as the human gives a cry.

Oh, baby; watch this eye squirt out the water from within,
Awfully slimy, I need some gin.
This blasted fork won't hold my breastbone,
Maybe, if I scrape the bits of flesh it would become the best ever known?

Snap, crack, and pop goes the great torso of my delight.
What a great taste these ribs make in the towers of the night.
Here we go Crypto, my lovely dog, take the heart.
It will cure your thirst and give you an early start.

Man, I'm awfully thirsty. I need some bloody Mary,
Young Mary wouldn't mind if I take her blood, you know the one from the dairy.
I must go into the night and go undercover.

Bye, Crypto, I'll be back by the full moon.
I'll bring the heart back for you soon.
The night comes to a close, for I must depart.
In the birth of the dawn the creatures of the night fall apart.

The poem "Terror of the night" is a poem I made describing the characters I use when I am using the email. I'm the type of person that loves quizzes and factual things that are very interesting. Over the years that I have been emailing my friends, I have used these characters to ask trivia questions to my friends and find out if they can get the answers. It's a little game that my friends and I play over the Internet. The main character's name is "The Trivia Kid". Many friends of mine have been frustrated in finding the answers to these trivia questions and have always loved receiving them through the email.

These characters are used in a humorous way to lighten up the mood so that my friends can concentrate on the question in the email. It is a sick kind of humor, but nonetheless it is a humor I use to challenge my friends. Usually I'll give them a time limit to find the answer and email it back to me.

Everybody in this time and age have ways to entertain them over the Internet. These characters happen to be my way of entertaining my friends. The Internet gives people the ability to look up all kinds of different things that you never knew existed. Trivia games are just part of the things I enjoy doing in my spare time. This poem was fun to write. It also reminds me of the fun I enjoy with my friends in trying to educate them with trivia questions.

BUGSY THE BUNNY

HIPPTY, HIPPTY HOP OFF INTO THE SUN,
MAN, OH, MAN IS THIS A HOT ONE.
EVERY TIME OF THE YEAR THEY TELL ME IT'S TIME,
TIME FOR WHAT, I ASK YOU IN MY RHYME.

WHO'S GONNA' HELP THE BUNNIES,
WHEN ALL MY EGGS ARE HONEY?
BUGSY A BUNNY WITH ATTITUDE, DUDE!
THE BUNNY WITH A SMILING CREW. THAT'S WHO!

BUGSY THE BUNNY, A BUNNY OF REACTION,
A BUNNY THAT IS READY FOR THE ACTION!
ONE, TWO, THREE,
ALL THE BUNNIES ARE FREE!

BUGSY WILL TAKE THE BASKET,
AND HIT THE EGGS WITH A RACKET.
ONE, TWO, THREE THEY'RE OUT OF HERE!
BUGSY THE BUNNY IS FIRING CAN'T YOU HEAR!

TONIGHT THE EGGS ARE GONE,
GONE INTO THE WIND OF A SONG.
MORNING COMES AND THE JOB IS DONE,
CHILDREN COME RUNNING FROM THE SUN.

RUN, BUGSY, RUN!
THE CHILDREN ARE AIMING FOR YOUR BUNS!
WHO CARES ABOUT THOSE EGGS! GET OUT OF THE SUN!
THEY'RE GONNA' TURN YOU INTO ONE!

"Bugsy the Bunny" was a poem that I had some fun with. It was Easter time and I was picturing a rabbit being forced into going from house to house to give Easter eggs out. I wondered what would happen if the Easter Bunny decided that he wasn't going to give out Easter eggs anymore. Out of that thought came this poem. If you imagine the way the poem is written, it's pretty funny. Our bunny, Bugsy, has decided not to give any more eggs to the children. He feels that they take him for granted. Bugsy waits in the morning sun to see the children's reaction to having no eggs in their baskets. Surprised by not having eggs the children decide to go running after Bugsy to get their eggs. Bugsy is force into running for his life as the children chase him into the forest. Bugsy realizes that this was a mistake and that he better find a hiding place before the children get him.

I always wondered why eggs came into the Easter holiday. As I wondered about this, the poem came into my mind and I wrote it down. Easter is a holiday to celebrate the resurrection of Christ. Where in the world did eggs come from? The reality is that eggs originated back in the days of the Egyptians and symbolized the birth of all living things. When Easter is celebrated the birth of all living things are celebrated as well, because of the resurrection of Jesus Christ. Bunny rabbits were added to the holiday as a fable for the children.

The poem "Bugsy the bunny" was a fun poem that was made to make people laugh at the Easter holiday. The poem showed a rabbit running away from the children after he had decided not to give any more eggs. It also shows that you can't always take things for granted. It was a funny poem that made me think why eggs were associated to the Easter Holiday.

Willow Tree

A pond stands near my soul,
Where an evergreen forest trumpets throughout the knoll.
Glimmering shadows of the rainbow dance through the night,
In hopes of capturing the stars' early light.

A tree stands before me crying for its sight,
A sight that horrendously distorts the figure in light.
Oh, Willow Tree, oh Willow Tree, don't cry it's just me,
Soon the emeralds of the world will soon shine on thee.

In all the heavens I called to be upon the mystery,
The mystery of Mother Nature's intense misery.
A misery to hold a body of great surrogate,
A change of form and mind enduring life's inner gate.

The poem "Willow Tree" was a poem that I wrote for fun. I based it on a tree that sat on the outside of my house at the time. It was just a poem that I wrote to practice with. I wanted to see if I could write a poem just by looking out the window and write about an object that didn't really mean anything to me. I think at one time or another we all tend to try to push ourselves to do different things just to see if we can live up to the challenge.

"Willow Tree" is one of the last poems in this book because it is an example of practicing to make perfect. We all have works like this one, no matter what they are. To me it shows that a person should always strive to be the best they can possibly be. It takes time and patience to make something come out right. The first time is never the best draft. Just as in life, perfection is achieved through hard work and determination; not easily attained.

With the poem "Willow Tree" ending my book, I must confess that the meaning of the work that went into it is what I want to leave with you. The idea that hard work and determination will result out of you challenging yourself. Don't give up the fight. Everybody is special in his or her own way. There is no such thing as perfection. Perfection is defined as achievement through hard work, determination, and the result of many mistakes.

Baby Bear

Walking down to the pond,
I am proud to be found.
Today is my first day that I go to have fun.
Watching fish as they wiggle, oh, how they wiggle about in the glass,
Like little children going off to class.

If I put my paw on one,
They scatter away from the sun.
Oh, how I wish to join all the fun.
If I stick my snout to the glass,
I can smell all the bass.

Uh, oh . . . I think my nose is stuck.
Help mom! I'm really stuck in this muck.
The little fishies seem to be laughing at all of the stuff.
You meanies, Stop laughing at me!
One day you'll be stuck to the sea.

Watch me laugh at all of you little fishies,
Thinking that I'm silly and stinky.
It's not like you smell any worse than Pinky,
My friend on the other side of the pond,
Even though she seems to always be singing a song.

Oh, hi Pinky.
I didn't mean you were stinky.
I was just mad at all of those little fishies.
Pinky, Pinky where are you going! I was just kidding
Kind' feel like I just got a licking.

Hi Mr. Fishy down below.
Think you can give a fella' a hard blow.
I'd appreciate it, you know.
Nuts, I'm stuck again.
Why doesn't anybody help me? It's not like I sinned?

Mom, you're here.
To free my snout from the / . . . Hey watch the ear!
How was I suppose to know about that . . . I was full of fear . . .
I'm sorry ma . . . . Hey, watch the ear . . . . help! I'm cut!
It seems mom won't be stopping because of my yelp. Ah nuts!

The poem "Baby Bear" is a poem I wrote thinking about children. Over the years I have learned children when growing up are very mischievous. They always seem to be getting into things. When I made the poem I was trying to illustrate the same behavior that a child would behave with the same incident that the bear goes through.

The poem became a rather silly and funny one just because of the silly circumstance that the bear finds himself in. At one time or another we as children have all allowed our curiosity to get the best of us. In this poem the baby bear allows his curiosity to get the best of him. The mother bear tries to teach the baby bear a lesson about curiosity and the dangers that will follow it by walking away from the baby bear in its time of need.

"Baby Bear" was a fun poem that I wrote to show the curiosity of children when they are growing up. It shows the results of curiosity can sometimes lead to. In this poem the old statement "Curiosity kills the cat" is redefined to "Curiosity kills the bear". A truly fun poem to write that at times has made me laugh. I hope you enjoy it.

ᴥA SPECIAL NOTEᴖ

In our lives it is rare that we run into lifetime friends that are true to you no matter what happens in your life. In the year 2002, a childhood friend of mine died. He was only 27 years old. He was my first friend when I was growing up in New Jersey. His father worked for Johnson & Johnson Company. When I was at the young age of 10 he moved away. Over the years we lost touch with each other and I occasionally was informed of how he was doing. In 2002, I was informed that he had died. Because his mother knew that we were childhood friends and that he had always thought of me, she gave me a poem that he wrote and a picture that he drew. The poem was called "The Colors of Life". The poem showed the colors of life; Green with abundance, Blue with Serenity, Purple with passion, Red with romance, Orange with overstanding, and Yellow with Transcendence. It showed that we must walk with faith in uncertain times and when life hands us pain and sorrow. Trouble times bring stronger minds. Don't ever forget that no matter what life brings you.

I came to a point in my life where I realized how important every moment in a person's life means so much. We should always let the ones we love know how much we really love them. You never know when your last day on Earth will be. I sometimes wonder if I had stayed in touch with him then he might not have died at such an early age.

_____ "He who leaves the light, dies by the wayside." _____

Christopher J. Kammerer (1975—2002)

"See you in Heaven my friend"

Printed in the United States
by Baker & Taylor Publisher Services